No Longer an Orphan

Freed by the Father's Love

Susan Dalla Corte

ii

DEDICATION

I dedicate this book to our Heavenly Father, who lovingly adopted me into His incredible family—His Family! To Jesus, the Son of God, my Beloved Savior and the Lord of my life, and to the Holy Spirit, whose daily guidance fills my journey with wisdom and peace. Your love and mercy renew my soul every single day.

CONTENTS

ACKNOWLEDGMENTS

Thank You, Lord, for helping me fulfill this call on my life to write my autobiography. It was out of obedience to you, Lord, that brought this book into being. Lord, You are so good in leading me to finish.

Thank you to my husband, Ken, for supporting me in writing this book. I so appreciate you! You were God's gift to me when I needed someone at a critical time in my life.

Thank you, Thierry Nakoa, a real brother in Christ who encouraged me to develop my skills. Thank you for creating this Scribal Course; I am grateful for your patience with me.

Thank you to my family, who have been a part of my life. I thank God for my first husband, Francis, who has since passed on to glory. I thank God for Shane, my beloved firstborn son. Thank you, Lord, for Luke and Joseph, my beloved sons who have passed on to glory. Thank you to my beautiful grandchildren, Aydin, Ivy, Logan, and Brody. Thank you, Laurie and Jen, my daughters-in-law, for bringing forth these precious children and being a part of our family.

CHAPTER ONE

My Early Years

I will not leave you comfortless:
I will come to you.—John 14:18 KJV

I was born into a family of 11 children. When I was very young, my mother divorced my father. Mom did not like my dad and blamed him for the divorce. My two brothers, Jim and Don, and I had the same parents, but we were not allowed to see my dad after the separation. I was four or five when I last saw him.

As I grew older, I discovered my mother had older children I wouldn't meet until later in life. My four older siblings, Pat, Henry, Nancy, and Herbert, had different dads from me and my two brothers. Soon after my mom left my dad, she met a man named Douglas. They married and had four more children together: Douglas, Robert, Carol, and Ronald.

My Mom did not want my two brothers and me around her. We were hidden in a closet or told to stay outside in the backyard when anyone came to our home. We were not to be seen. She had some mental and emotional issues, perhaps from childhood trauma. She would not discuss anything about her past with anyone. At this time, we were living in New London, Connecticut. Jim, Don, and I would be left outside to fend for ourselves. Jim would always steal from the milk, bread, and ice cream trucks so we had something to eat. We would go behind grocery stores to dig in the garbage to find what food we could. My older sister Nancy would babysit us when our mother and stepdad left for the weekend to go to Massachusetts with the younger children. At the time, my stepdad was in the Navy. When he got his pay, he would come home drunk. Once, we were all in bed, and he broke down the front door, yelling for us to come down and get some ice cream. We were a bit scared, and so was our mom. I remember not knowing whether to comply or not. We went downstairs frightened because we knew we would be in trouble if we didn't.

My mother was caught abusing us by a neighbor who turned her in to the police. She even asked him if he could take us. However, as a single man in the Navy, it would not have worked out. Shortly after this, my parents were arrested for child abuse. This was a time of separation from our family. I would not see my mom and stepdad until I became older.

When my father and my mother forsake me, then the LORD will take me up (Psalm 27:10 KJV).

A New Family

Don, Jim, and I went to live with the Willand family. We called them Mom and Dad. My foster sister, Helen, was three then, and I was seven. We lived with them for about a year and a half. The family lived in Groton, Connecticut. I was skinny and anemic when we were brought to this new home. I was fed liver and beet hash to up my iron levels. It was not the tastiest meal I ever had, but it helped me get better. We were taught about the Bible. I learned Psalms 23 and 100 and all the names of the Bible in order. My brothers, Jim and Don, were not as excited as I was to learn about the Bible.

My foster sister was an only child and did not like the fact I had moved in, and she was a bit angry about it. She was jealous and felt we were taking her place. At this young age, I did not know that there were evil beings that influenced children to do naughty things. She would cause trouble, but I would be blamed for it. Once, my foster mom was looking for the Bible storybook she would read to us every night. She went looking for it, but it was nowhere to be found. Helen told her I was the last one to have it. The truth was I did not have it, nor did I know where it was. They believed Helen but not me. We all looked for it but could not find it. I was told I would be punished for lying if I did not find it when I got home from school. I went to school that day with a pit of fear in my stomach. I did not want to go home for fear of not finding the book because I knew I did not know where it was.

I feared being disciplined, so I decided to run away as I walked home from school. It was a sunny but cold February afternoon, and snow was on the ground. After it turned dark, I decided to head back home. As I was walking, a police car pulled up and asked me if I was okay. The Officer was a friend of the family and attended our church. She talked me into getting in the car to take me home. When I got back, my foster mom was crying. She asked me why I ran away. I told her I did not know where the Bible storybook was and that I did not have it. She told me during the day she found it; It had been underneath a pile of clothes on a chair in her bedroom. She felt terrible and apologized for not believing me. I forgave her and received a big hug from her and my foster dad. Helen also apologized for lying to her parents and hugged me, too! This began a deeper love for one another.

A short time went on, and my foster parents realized my brother Jim had a lot of emotional problems because of the abuse he had endured from our mother. They decided they could not handle him because of his behavioral issues. The State of Connecticut removed him and put him in another placement we were not familiar with. Don and I would stay a little longer. I completed first and second grade, and Mom and Dad Willand did a lot to get Don and me up to grade level. Both of my foster parents were teachers. My foster mom took care of us and did not teach while we were at their home. My foster Dad was an elementary teacher and in the Air Force Reserves. He also worked at Electric Boat as a night guard during the summers. This was in 1957-1958. We were allowed to watch new submarines being launched. It was pretty exciting.

We were pleasantly surprised when Don and I were told the Willand's wanted to adopt us! My foster parents went to the State of Connecticut to obtain permission to do so. A social worker visited us to ask how we were being treated. Don and I were not at all fond of this lady. She did not want us to be adopted by a Christian family. My foster parents had 200 signatures from friends and family to support the adoption, but the court denied the request. Our stay was short-lived, and we left with the sadness of not knowing where we would live. I missed this home, and I didn't understand everything at that time. Sometimes, things do not always work out the way we want. We were fond of this family.

While there, we received lovely birthday and Christmas gifts, visited relatives in Maine and New Hampshire, vacationed in Niagara Falls, took a boat ride under the falls, and saw the colored lights at night. What beauty the Lord God shared with us in creating Niagara Falls. I got to see the glory of God.

We also rode the train up Mount Washington in New Hampshire. It was quite a ride as it rattled back and forth. I was a bit afraid while it was chugging up that great mountain. It was very cold and 32 degrees in July at the top! I will forever be thankful to the Willands for showing us love for the first time.

> *We know that all things work together for good to them that love God, to them who are called according to His purpose.* Romans 8:28a KJV

My Time in an Orphanage

Our next move was to an orphanage in Warehouse Point, Connecticut. It was called the Connecticut State Receiving Home. There were four dorms on the property, one for girls aged seven to 16, where I lived, and one for boys aged seven to nine, where Don lived. We had discovered our older brother Jim lived in the dorm for 10–12-year-olds. And there was a dorm for 13–16-year-old boys. This meant I was now with both brothers. We were at least on the same property but only saw each other for Saturday and Sunday recreation time. Two housemothers were assigned to each dorm. We were given new clothes, dungarees, t-shirts and penny loafers. We all got to look like each other! We were treated well but had to help scrub showers, mop floors, and clean at a young age. This taught me a good work ethic at a young age. There was little Christian education there, and we only attended church on Easter and Christmas.

It was at this orphanage where I discovered my love for horses. While at the orphanage, a family brought ponies for the children to ride. They came to my dorm first and offered us a ride. When it was my turn, I was excited and did not want it to end. The ponies were beautiful and brought me such joy. It awakened my love for horses. My Mom also had a passion for horses. I found out later that my brother Henry had trained horses professionally. Little did I know that horses would also become a part of my future.

> *Hast thou given the horse strength? Hast thou clothed his neck with thunder? Canst thou make him afraid as a grasshopper? The glory of his nostrils is terrible.— Job 39:19-20*

The orphanage was good to us. They took us to the beach and ball games; we enjoyed movie nights on Fridays and dances on Saturday nights. The dances would be held outside in the parking lot in the summer, and the older girls would teach me new dance moves. I learned how to do the twist, the bop, and other dances. We attended school on the property, and I completed grades 3 and 4. During the Christmas season, Jim, Don, and I were invited to a home with a family with no children for a weekend. They bought us Christmas gifts and made us feel special, and we enjoyed our time together. Here again, the Lord was watching over us.

My brother Jim was taken away from the orphanage not long after. They took him to a boy's school in New York for exceptional help. Jim, Don, and I were separated once again. Soon, a new social worker, Mr. K, visited Don and me. We were asked what type of foster home we would like, and I immediately spoke up and asked for a farm with horses. In August 1961, the orphanage set off to Camp Ayo Po in Somers, Connecticut, for three weeks. Ayo Po is a Native Indian word meaning "I have joy." I had great joy as I learned to fish, swim, and row a boat!

We also did arts and crafts and bunked in cabins in the woods with young college counselors as our leaders. I helped in the kitchen and set the tables. One day, I had a horrible experience with some of the girls in my cabin. One of the girls had gotten sick, and they blamed me, saying I was the cause of her sickness. They were mean and relentless, calling me nasty names. I ran out of the cabin and down the dirt road, and no one tried to stop me. The counselor was not around then, so off I went with my little wounded heart. I found a field of cows and went in, but the cows came toward me, and I quickly exited back to the dirt road, afraid of their size. I grew tired, so I turned around to go back to camp. The counselors had realized I was missing and notified the police, who found me and picked me up. I was feeling so rejected! This was just another layer on my already rejected, broken heart. We were at this camp for about two weeks when Mr. K came and told Don and me, we were leaving to go to a new foster home, a farm in the country. Boy, was I ever excited! My heart was so pleased!

And whoso shall receive one such little child in my name receives me. Matt. 18:5-KJV

Living Life on a Farm

They sent us to our new home when I was 10. We rode with Mr. K for what seemed like forever before arriving at our destination. We were on our way to a farm with horses and ponies! Our new foster parents, Mr. and Mrs. Bunker, were an older couple. Curious children ran to the car to see the newcomers as we pulled into the yard. The youngest girl, who was seven, informed me that I was only there to play with her. That did not go over well with me. But things would get rough at times between her and me. She wanted to play house and dolls, but I only wanted to be around the horses. Yes! There were horses, ponies, cows, pigs, chickens, dogs, cats, and kids. Three other girls lived here, one my age and two in their teens. My brother Don and six other boys also comprised 11 children at the house. Sometimes there would be more. Eight children in the home were the Bunker's grandchildren, and the rest were foster children. We were taught various jobs and responsibilities. The girls helped Nana, aka Mrs. Bunker, clean the house, do dishes, do laundry, and cook. The boys' jobs were to fill wood boxes and help Grandpa, aka

Mr. Bunker, milk the cows, clean the stalls, and feed the calves, pigs, and chickens.

We worked hard but also had time to ride the ponies and play baseball after school and on weekends when there was spare time. However, work and homework always came first; there was only playtime if we finished our chores or homework. My foster sister Linda was my age and taught me how to ride bareback on King, the Shetland stallion. I had excellent balance and could ride quite well without falling off. The Lord knew how much I loved horses and riding. He was the one who put that passion inside of me. Linda and I would ride on Saturdays and go for miles. My other foster sister, Cheryl, was younger and wanted me to stay and play with her. This was very challenging for me. Sometimes, Nana would tell me to play with Cheryl, but my heart was not into it. Sometimes, we got along, and other times we did not. Once we were fighting, Nana broke us up and told us to stand in the middle of the kitchen floor and rub our noses together. You can only imagine how that went! But we had to do so until Nana said to stop. Neither of us enjoyed that, so we did not fight as often.

In fifth grade, I needed a new pair of shoes for school. Nana's daughter, Bernise, bought me a pair of red shoes with buckles. They were too big, and I wouldn't say I liked the color or the buckles. I complained and exclaimed, "I hate these shoes!" Nana told Bernise to put them back in the box and return them to the store. Nana said that since I was so ungrateful, I would wear whatever used shoes were available, a pair of boy's slippers. Yes, boy's slippers! So, I went to school in a pair of boy's slippers for two weeks. Talk about humble pie. That wasn't the end of the story. While playing kickball, I kicked the ball hard, and my slipper flew in the air! Everyone was laughing but me. God has a way of teaching us not to be proud or thankless.

I was in fifth grade when I met my best friend, Sharon. I would spend weekends with her. She had lost her mom to an illness, so her dad was raising her and her three sisters on his own. Her dad met a lady a few years later who had five sons, and they married when I was 12. I was drawn to her stepbrother, Francis. He was kind to Sharon and me. When I stayed at her home, I always asked Francis to give us rides to different places. We would wear his flannel shirts when we got chilly. He would always joke around with us and was always joyful. Sharon was his favorite stepsister, so he didn't mind giving us rides when needed. Later, Sharon asked me if I wanted to vacation with the family at the beach. Of course, I wanted to! I excitedly packed up and went off with Sharon and her family. All the girls stayed in one tent, and the guys, who were all older, stayed in their tents. We were in our teens, and the guys were in their late teens and early twenties. I developed a crush on Francis while at that beach. I was only 14, so he was not interested in me; I was too young and immature. We often experience emotions that are not under our control as teenagers.

One weekend, I rode one of the horses, Princess, bareback to Sharon's house, hoping to see her and Francis. Neither one was home, so I headed back to my house. Back in the 1960s, it was safe to ride on the roads of Lebanon without worrying about traffic. People were pretty kind about giving horses the right of way. As I got closer to home, I cantered the horse on the side of the road, where there was plenty of space away from traffic. As I got closer to home, I tried to slow down, but to no avail; Princess was anxious to get home. I pulled the reins, but she just picked up the pace. We had to cross a two-lane highway to get to my street, and Princess was at a fast gallop by then. She turned quickly to cross the road, but it was slippery, and she fell in the middle of the road on top of me. She was able to get up uninjured, but my leg was badly hurt. Of course, this meant a trip to the ER.

I had to use crutches for 6 weeks, which took a toll on me. Thinking back, I know I should not have gone looking for Francis. At this young and vulnerable age, parental advice would have been beneficial in helping me control my emotions and not chase after a boy. Francis became friends with my foster brother Bill, and they would work on cars together. He was dating other girls, and I was a bit jealous. As I grew older, other fellas asked me out, but I was not interested at all. Francis would come over, and we would sit and talk about life. When I turned 16, Francis finally asked me out on a date, and Nana allowed it! We would go to the coffee shop with Bill and over to his home to visit his mom and family. We also went to his Aunt Mary and Uncle Joe's farm to swim and have picnics.

In March of 1968, when I turned 17, we discussed getting married. Francis bought me a diamond ring, and we set a date of August 3rd, 1968. Nana went along with it, but she was not happy about it. I had a new female social worker because Mr. K retired. I do not remember her name, but she was only 22. She thought it was a "great" idea for me to get married, which meant there would be one less child in the welfare system. She also was getting married at the same time. But Fran's mom did not like the idea at all! She thought I was too young and immature, but we won this battle. We got married on August 3, 1968. I may not have gotten married so young if the Lord had been involved. But God allows us to make our own choices.

CHAPTER TWO

A Young Bride

O But from the beginning of the creation God made them male and female. For this cause shall a man leave his father and mother, and cleave to his wife. Mark 10::7 KJV

O ur wedding took place on a hot, humid, muggy day with plenty of sunshine in Lebanon, Connecticut, at two in the afternoon at the Congregational Church. The wedding reception was outdoors on our farm with 200 honored guests who witnessed us become Mr. and Mrs. Francis Drum. Everything went according to plan, and it was beautiful! We had a lovely time with the guests, music, and food. We left our gifts to be opened when we returned from our honeymoon. We left the reception for the White Mountains in New Hampshire. That night, we did not get the bridal suite we had hoped for but ended up in a small motel with few amenities. We spent the next night in a nicer motel with a honeymoon suite. We went hiking up the Flume Gorge and visited the "Old Man of the Mountain," which is no longer there. I was homesick, so we did not stay long, only three days. We headed to our home in a small apartment in Lebanon, Connecticut, where we began our life together. As an auto mechanic, I thought my husband would go to work and then come home to spend time with me. But that was not the case, and being a young wife, I had much to learn.

Francis had a kind heart, and many people took advantage of this. He chose to take calls about vehicles and automotive problems instead of spending time with me when he got home. Every evening after supper, he would rush off to assist anyone in need. Upon returning back home, he would unwind by watching some television before eventually retiring to bed for the night. We did not spend much time together. Remember, I was still in high school back then. Juggling school and chores was tough, but I managed. Since I didn't get my drivers license until I was 22, I had to rely on the bus. Waking up early for the bus would eat into our time.

Three months after getting married, Francis's family and friends went on a hunting trip without us ladies. They stayed a week, and we joined them on the last weekend. Fran and I missed each other. We spent time together and conceived our first son, Shane. It was November of 1968, and I was allowed to stay in school until April of 1969. I would finish my schoolwork at home and hand it in each week. I was now 18 years old. Shane was due on August 3, 1969, but came on July 11, 1969. I thank God he came early. I was underweight when I conceived him, and it took a lot out of me. It would have been more difficult if I had to wait until his due date of August 3rd, which happened to be our 1st wedding anniversary. It was not an easy delivery. He had a broken collarbone and weighed six pounds and four ounces.

As Shane was born in the summer of 1969, I had some time to be with him before I started my senior year of high school. I did not want to return, but Fran encouraged me to complete the school year. Nana and Fran's mom, Ruth, babysat so I could finish, and I graduated in June of 1970. Boy was I ever glad I was done with school! Shane was two years old when my second son, Luke, was born on August 5th, 1971. I did not know what lay ahead with raising a son with disabilities.

CHAPTER THREE

Family Challenges with a Disabled Child

""In my distress I cried unto the LORD, and he heard me." Psalms 120:1-KJV

By this time, I was out of school and had graduated. I was eating a good diet with lots of organic foods, believing this would bring forth a healthy baby. But this was not the case for Luke or me. After Luke was born, I would try to nurse him, but he would not respond as a regular baby would. He would cry and push away from being nursed. I then decided to bottle feed instead, but the formula did not agree with him. Luke would scream and experience terrible pain after he took his formula. He did not sit up until he was nine months old or walk until he was three. Luke was non-verbal and diagnosed with autism and mental delay at the age of two. His hips were not lined up correctly, and he had to wear braces while sleeping for about six months. In the meantime, our family moved from Lebanon to Colchester, Connecticut, and I soon conceived our third child. Joseph was born on August 7th, 1974. Luke was three and able to walk, but his hyperactivity made it difficult to control him. He would get into trouble and had to be watched constantly. I had to place locks on all the cupboards, cabinets, closet doors, and refrigerator. He would open jars and dump whatever was in them. It wasn't easy to get babysitters so I could get a break, and it was hard on the few we could get, as well as on Shane and Joseph.

My husband worked two jobs to support our growing family, leaving him with little time to help at home. Managing Luke's behavior placed significant stress on the entire family. We lived in a two-bedroom house where Luke shared a room with Shane. Many nights, Luke would wake up and jump on Shane, disturbing his sleep.

I eventually gave Luke his own room, locking the door at night to keep him from waking everyone prematurely. His behavior took a toll on both Shane and Joseph. I often asked Shane to watch Luke for a few minutes, but it was never easy. The boys tried to play with him, but Luke couldn't sit still for long. He especially loved playing in the sandpile, running his hands through the sand and putting it in his hair.

I sincerely appreciated Shane and Fran for stepping in whenever they could give me much-needed breaks. Joseph also did his best to entertain Luke, but the stress was difficult to manage. Nana gave the boys a pony named Mitzie, bringing them great joy. Mitzie seemed to understand that Luke was different. She allowed him to crawl under her belly without harming him—animals have an incredible sense of such things.

We fenced off a portion of the yard to prevent Luke from running into the road, as we lived on a poultry farm. Despite our precautions, he once contracted salmonella after putting his fingers in his mouth following playtime in the dirt. He had to be hospitalized for two weeks. Keeping Luke safe was a constant and exhausting challenge.

Eventually, I reached out to the State of Connecticut for help. They arranged for someone to come for a few hours in the evenings a few times a week so I could prepare meals without interruptions. Francis also built a gate between the kitchen and living room to keep Luke out while we cooked. Mealtimes required extra effort, as Luke had to be fed separately to stop him from grabbing food off his brothers' plates.

As Luke grew older, managing him became even harder. He was bigger, stronger, and increasingly difficult to handle. His uncontrollable energy and frantic behavior caused significant stress for everyone. He ran wildly around the house, leaving us all at wit's end. I became hyper-vigilant, always listening for any movement during the night. Shane and Joseph also struggled, often unable to sleep well due to the constant tension.

Through it all, Shane showed remarkable maturity and love for his younger brother. I am deeply grateful for how he helped Luke at such a young age. Shane and Joseph displayed incredible courage and compassion, even when the situation was difficult. Being a caretaker is a demanding and exhausting role, and it affects the entire family. Without adequate support, it's easy to become overwhelmed, tired, and irritable—even when you don't mean to be.

We eventually began searching for a preschool that could accommodate a special needs child. During this time, I found great comfort in prayer, and verses from the book of Psalms became a source of strength.

> *"I love the Lord, because he hath heard my voice and my supplications. Because he hath inclined his ear unto me, therefore will I call upon as long as I live."* Psalm 116: 1-2 -KJV

We eventually searched for a preschool that accommodated special needs children and found one in Manchester, Connecticut. Luke went to school for four hours daily, giving me a little break. Since he couldn't talk, they started teaching him sign language. The school had special teachers and equipment to help him in a calm, controlled environment. Unfortunately, he aged out of the program at seven, and we had to find a new school for him, which became our next big challenge.

The public school in Colchester didn't have the teachers or classrooms needed to help kids like Luke. They told us they couldn't do anything for him. In the early 1970s, there weren't many schools for children with special needs. So, we began searching for a school that could take Luke. The State of Connecticut's Department of Child and Youth Services helped us. My husband, Francis, and I visited schools in Connecticut, Rhode Island, and Massachusetts but couldn't find anything.

Finally, we heard about a special school in Devereux, Pennsylvania. The town of Colchester didn't want to pay for Luke's education outside of Connecticut, but the court decided in our favor. The State agreed to cover his room and board, but only if we gave up custody of Luke to them. It was heartbreaking. We didn't have the money, and Luke's needs were too much for us to handle alone. We had to do what was best for him, even though it was one of the hardest decisions we ever made.

I fell into a deep depression, and Francis was struggling too. He started drinking at night to help him relax and sleep. Letting Luke go felt like losing a part of our family.

Francis and I took Luke to the school in Pennsylvania with a social worker from the State. After Luke was accepted, we packed his things, and the social worker took him to the school. It broke my heart. It reminded me of when I was seven and taken from my family. I'm sure Luke didn't understand what was happening. The school had a rule that parents couldn't visit for a month so the kids could adjust to being away from home. It was an adjustment for us as well.

Luke came home for three weeks during summer, as well as on Christmas and spring breaks. Life became less stressful in some ways, but it still wasn't easy. When he came home, it was hard for the family to adjust. We had to stay alert at all times because Luke wasn't in control of himself. At eight, he started having seizures. He took medication to manage his seizures, but sometimes they still occurred.

Luke attended that school for five years. During that time, his seizures got worse. He had both grand mal and petit mal seizures that sometimes lasted an hour. When Luke turned 12, the school decided he should leave because he wasn't making progress and his health was declining. We couldn't care for him at home, so the State placed him in a new facility in Connecticut. At least this time, he was closer to us, and we could visit him on weekends.

By then, I had started working full-time as a paraprofessional in the Colchester school system. Luke's health problems continued. He was hospitalized with meningitis, but thank God, he recovered. He often got pneumonia because he had trouble swallowing, and food would go into his lungs. Most of what he had learned in school was lost because of his seizures. Doctors tried different medications, but his seizures were hard to control. They said Luke was one in 100 children with such severe seizure disorders.

In November 2012, Luke got pneumonia again and was hospitalized for two weeks. He wasn't eating much and lost a lot of weight. After being sent back to his group home, he was readmitted a week later with double pneumonia. The doctor suggested moving him to a rehab center where he could get better care. I signed the papers, and Luke was moved to a center in Marlborough, Connecticut, where I lived.

I started visiting Luke every day. He was put on hospice care because he wasn't eating and was losing too much weight. We didn't think he would live much longer. But God had other plans. After four months, Luke started eating again, and his weight slowly returned. I kept visiting him daily, praying with him, and playing Christian TV programs to create a peaceful atmosphere. I also took him outside in his wheelchair for fresh air.

This became my routine for 10 years. Having Luke nearby was a blessing because I didn't have to travel far to see him. While this journey was full of pain and challenges, it also taught me about faith, love, and the strength God gives us to keep going.

> *"Have I not commanded you? Be strong and courageous. Do not be afraid; do not be discouraged, for the LORD your God will be with wherever you go." Joshua 1:9 –KJV*

CHAPTER FOUR

My Time in a Legalistic Church

"O foolish Galatians, who hath bewitched you, that ye should not obey the truth, before whose eyes Jesus Christ hath been evidently set forth, crucified among you? This only would I learn of you, received ye the Spirit by works of the law, or by the hearing of faith?"—Galatians 3:1-2 KJV

In November 1968, I saw a free religious magazine ad in Reader's Digest. I was 18 years old and decided to send for it. The magazine talked a lot about current events and made me very fearful. I needed to get saved before the Lord returned, so I gave my life to Him.

The church I joined taught that Saturday was the only day of worship, and we had to follow it strictly. We couldn't do dishes or any work from Friday to Saturday sunset. We followed the Sabbath and the dietary laws in the Old Testament. On Saturdays, we only went to church or visited others for fellowship. We didn't celebrate Christmas, Easter, or birthdays, which was hard on my family. I helped shop and wrap Christmas gifts for them but didn't give or receive gifts myself.

We were taught that ours was the only true church and were told not to read any literature besides what the church provided. They didn't believe in the Trinity or understand who the Holy Spirit was.

I attended church once a month for a long time because it was two and a half hours away. I didn't have a driver's license, so my friends went out of their way to pick me up and drop me off. Sometimes, I brought my children with me if my husband gave his permission.

Not everything about the church was bad. We had good fellowship and shared meals. We observed the Passover and Holy Days, which brought blessings. I learned a lot about the Bible and other topics, especially the end times. We tithed and gave special offerings, and I saw blessings even if some teachings were incorrect.

Every fall, we saved money to celebrate the Feast of Tabernacles. It felt like a vacation. I took the children when I could. There were meetings and activities like horseback riding, eating out, visiting historical sites, and enjoying outdoor fun. Luke came with me when he was younger, but it wasn't easy. At first, we only stayed a few days. Later, when Luke went to a special school, I took Shane and Joseph with me. Francis usually stayed home to work, though he joined us a few times at places like Lake George, the Cape, and the Pocono Mountains, where we rented cabins.

I was part of this church for over 30 years. When Joseph turned 10, he didn't want to attend anymore, so Francis had me get a babysitter for him. Shane stopped attending at 17. A few years later, I realized it was time to leave, too. The strictness of the church had made me hard and harsh, which wasn't easy on my family. We had good times, but it was challenging. Shane attended some youth activities and proms through the church, and we met many friendly people and enjoyed their company. But my long church days—leaving early and returning late—took a toll on my marriage.

When the church leader passed away in 1992, everything started to change. The new leader apologized for things that had gone wrong in the past. We learned we weren't the only true church, as we'd been taught. Sunday worship was allowed, but the church didn't understand the Holy Spirit or His purpose. By 1998, I was no longer satisfied and decided to leave.

After leaving, I began attending a church closer to home. There, I was introduced to the Holy Spirit and His power. I cried out to God, wanting to know Him, not just about Him. He answered my prayer. Jeremiah 29:13 stands out to me: "And ye shall seek me, and find me, when ye shall search for me with all your heart."

This marked the start of my new journey, building a deeper relationship with the Lord instead of just following religion. Praise His Holy Name! I visited different churches, searching for the "perfect one," but I've learned there's no perfect church because there are no perfect people. Go where the Holy Spirit leads—you'll feel peace in your spirit when you're in the right place.

Looking back, my time in the legalistic church impacted my family and me. It was one of the reasons Francis turned to alcohol, even after Luke left. He became an alcoholic and wasn't ready to stop until 19 years later.

CHAPTER FIVE

Living With an Alcoholic

"And be not drunk with wine, wherein is excess; but be filled with the Spirit." Eph. 5:18 KJV

I can only imagine how hard things were for Francis. He was under so much pressure—

raising a special needs child, working demanding jobs, and dealing with a wife (me) who wasn't always supportive. He didn't have much self-confidence, but he worked very hard and was liked by so many people. He had a kind heart and was easy to get along with. At this time, I was still attending the Saturday Church.

When Francis came home, the drinking started. He wasn't a mean drunk—he was friendly and funny, often joking around and making others laugh. But his father had also been an alcoholic, and unlike Francis, his father was mean when he drank. Alcohol was always present at family gatherings, and over time, Francis' drinking got worse. He began hiding whiskey bottles, which I'd find while cleaning, and he frequently stopped at the package store.

On Friday nights, Francis started going to bars. I stayed home because my church beliefs wouldn't allow me to go out. Francis would come home drunk, often after midnight. I began attending Al-Anon meetings, hoping to learn how to cope. I didn't realize then that I was part of the problem, too.

As the drinking worsened, accidents became common—car crashes, falls, and other troubles. Francis was also smoking three packs of cigarettes a day, and by age 38, he had his first heart attack. He couldn't work anymore, and our family struggled. I wasn't working full-time, and we had to rely on welfare for a short time. I tried doing housecleaning jobs, but it wasn't enough to support us. Even then, Francis kept drinking, and I was at my breaking point.

I lost all my pride and cried out to God. I told the Lord, "Either sober my husband up or help me raise my sons, Shane and Joseph, without him." That's when I heard God speak to my spirit, saying, "You need to apologize for your part in his drinking."

I obeyed. I sat down with Francis and apologized for the ways I had contributed to his drinking. I told him it wasn't all his fault. Then I told him he had one month to decide: either get sober or continue drinking. If he chose to drink, we would separate, and I would raise the children alone. He didn't like that, but I was firm. I told him that if he chose sobriety, he would need to enroll in a program.

A month later, the day came, and I asked him for his decision. We had already arranged for a program if he chose to go. Francis agreed to attend but wanted one last drink before leaving. I poured the booze down the sink, which didn't make him happy, but he packed up and left for the program.

The program lasted a month. We couldn't see him for the first week, and he couldn't come home until graduation. By God's grace, he graduated—praise the Lord!

The first Friday Francis was back home, he went to an Alcoholics Anonymous meeting. That evening, I decided to take a ride on my horse, Poncho. It was September 7, 1989. I told my sons, Shane (15) and Joseph (10) that I'd be back soon. I saddled Poncho and set off down the road around 7 PM, planning to ride through a favorite trail in the woods.

With Poncho ready to go, I climbed on and started down the road, looking forward to a nice ride. But as I went deeper into the woods, the path became hard to follow. Someone had cut down trees, leaving branches blocking the trail, and there were deep ruts from heavy equipment.

The sunlight was fading quickly, and I realized the trail was too dangerous to continue. It was dark now, and I couldn't find my way home. Feeling scared, I decided to unsaddle Poncho and spend the night in a small clearing. I found a spot, sat on my saddle pad, and suddenly, a little mouse darted out, scolding me for sitting near its hole. I hadn't seen it before because of the thick brush. It made me laugh—God sure has a sense of humor! I moved my pad to a new spot to give the mouse its space.

The night was cold, and I wasn't dressed warmly. As the hours passed, I heard voices in the distance. A policeman was searching nearby, but he couldn't hear me calling out. It must have been close to 11 p.m. The moon was bright, but it was still very dark. I tried to rest, but then I heard an animal creeping closer. It was bigger than a mouse—maybe a raccoon? I yelled, "Don't come any closer!" and it turned away.

While sitting there, I thought about how unwise I had been to take this ride. Still, I knew God was with me. Back then, I didn't fully understand how the Holy Spirit guides us, but I could feel God's presence.

Later, Poncho began pacing nervously, snorting with wide, bulging eyes. A loud crackle came from the woods, and I quickly grabbed his reins to calm him. Though I couldn't see the creature, I suspected it was a large deer. Thankfully, it ran off, and Poncho stayed with me. I was incredibly grateful he didn't get loose and leave me alone in the woods.

As the sun began to rise, I saddled Poncho, prayed for safety, and trusted God to guide us out. Poncho led the way, and we made it out without any problems. My neighbor Norma and her friend met me at the road. Norma took Poncho home while her friend drove me back to my house. By the time I got home around 7 a.m., I was completely exhausted.

My family was waiting for me in the kitchen, along with the police sergeant, who had been preparing to start another search. A local pastor had prayed Psalm 23 over my family during the night:

"The LORD is my shepherd; I shall not want. He maketh me to lie down in green pastures; He leadeth me beside the still waters. He restoreth my soul: He leadeth me in the paths of righteousness for His name's sake. Yea, though I walk through the valley of the shadow of death, I will fear no evil: for thou art with me; thy rod and thy staff they comfort me. Thou preparest a table before me in the presence of mine enemies: thou anoint my head with oil; my cup runneth over. Surely goodness and mercy shall follow me all the days of my life: and I will dwell in the house of the Lord for ever."

I'm sure Francis was very worried, not knowing where Poncho and I were. It must have been hard for him, especially since it was his first week home after finishing his program. Thankfully, everything turned out well. The story even made it into the *New London Day* newspaper.

CHAPTER SIX

Fran's Many Life Challenges with His Health

"O LORD, thou hast brought up my soul from the grave: Thou hast kept me alive, that I should not go down to the pit. - Psalm 30:3

Francis had stopped drinking, but he continued smoking. Over time, we noticed he was losing weight, and it was getting harder for him to breathe. He went to a cardiologist, who advised him to see a stomach specialist because of the weight loss. The cardiologist also said Francis had a weak heart and angina but wouldn't recommend heart surgery since he was still smoking. Essentially, the doctor told Francis his life was at serious risk.

Following the advice, Francis visited a stomach specialist, but they couldn't find the cause of the weight loss. The specialist referred him to another doctor at Farmington Medical Center, who discovered that Francis wasn't getting enough blood flow to his stomach, which prevented him from digesting food properly. This doctor sent him to a cardiologist at the same center; we'll call him Dr. Sam.

Dr. Sam ran tests and found three complete blockages in Francis's heart. He urgently recommended bypass surgery. Francis was only 42 years old at the time. This was the moment he finally quit smoking—for good. He never picked up another cigarette again. I praise God for guiding us to a doctor who didn't give up on Francis.

Francis underwent a five-bypass surgery at Saint Francis Hospital. Initially planned to last five hours, the procedure was completed in three hours. That was God's work! The surgery was successful and extended Francis's life by 25 years. Before the operation, we were anxious because his health was so poor that we weren't sure he would survive the wait. But God gave me peace, and He provided us with the best surgeon at the time.

When Francis turned 60, he needed surgery to repair a hernia. Before the procedure, a cardiologist found an aneurysm near his heart. Despite the risk, they determined his heart was strong enough for surgery. Both the hernia and aneurysm were successfully repaired, although the recovery was challenging. Francis endured pain and breathing issues due to his diaphragm being pushed into his lungs during the operation. Still, we were grateful he made it through another major surgery.

After recovering, Francis could only work part-time, so he got a maintenance job at a senior living complex in our town. However, another major incident happened in the fall of 2008.

While at work, his boss asked him to stand in a tractor bucket and be lifted about 15 feet to cut a tree limb. The driver accidentally hit a rock, jolting the tractor and causing Francis to fall. He hit his head and landed on a rock, crushing the bottom of his foot. At the ER, he waited in excruciating pain for 10 hours before being treated. X-rays revealed that his foot was severely damaged—crushed like gravel. They put a cast on it, but the cast caused a third-degree burn on his ankle and didn't help with the injury.

Francis spent two weeks in the ICU as his body began to shut down. He was in critical condition, with tubes everywhere. I worked during the day and visited him in the evenings. By God's grace, his body began to heal, though the pain from the foot injury remained intense. After three weeks of rehab, he came home, but the nerve damage in his heel left him in chronic pain. Francis relied on a walker and later a cane for mobility.

Through it all, I am thankful to God for saving my husband again. Despite all these trials, God's hand has been with us every step of the way!

CHAPTER SEVEN

The Reunion with My Birth Mother

"Put on therefore. As the elect of God, holy and beloved, bowels of mercies, kindness, humbleness of mind, meekness, longsuffering; forbearing one another, and forgiving one another, if any man have a quarrel against any: even as Christ forgave you, so also do ye."
—Colossians 3:12-13 KJV.

In 2003, I received a call from my birth mother. She had moved from El Cajon, California, to

New Hampshire with my stepdad, Douglas, who I called Dad by then. Douglas was the man my mother married after leaving my birth father. I learned that Dad's daughter, Charlene, from his first marriage, had invited them to move in with her and her family because she didn't think they should live alone at their age. Charlene and her husband, Mike, lived in a large house with their daughter, Jenny, so there was plenty of space.

That year, my parents and Charlene invited Fran and me to visit them for Thanksgiving dinner. We accepted and made the trip to New Hampshire. I was surprised by the invitation since I hadn't heard much from my mom over the years. But I realized that God was giving me a chance to reconnect with her for the few years she had left on earth.

At the time, Dad was still able to drive, so they later came down to visit Fran and me. My sons were grown and living on their own by then. I invited Mom and Dad to visit during my vacation time since I worked in the local school system and had breaks during spring, summer, Thanksgiving, and Christmas. They spent many holidays with us, and I cherished those moments.

One day, God told me to ask my mom for forgiveness for anything I had done to hurt her and to forgive her for anything she had done to hurt me. When the moment came, I followed God's instruction. My mom didn't say much—she seemed surprised. But then, she took off a beautiful gold ring, handed it to me, and said, "This belongs to you." That simple act marked the beginning of a healing process in my life. It was a moment of growth for both of us. The Bible teaches us to forgive, and I experienced firsthand how much healing comes from obedience to God's Word. Ephesians 4:32 says, "And be ye kind one to another, tenderhearted, forgiving one another, even as God for Christ's sake hath forgiven you."

In spring of 2007, my mom began experiencing severe back pain and was admitted to a hospital in New Hampshire for surgery. Dad and I stayed in a motel nearby to be close to her during her recovery. She wanted to be closer to home, so she was transferred to a hospital near Hudson, New Hampshire. During her stay, she developed a deep bedsore that wouldn't heal. Mom came home to recover. Around the same time, a bad ice storm hit New Hampshire so Mom and Dad came to stay with us during this time.

It was Christmas vacation, so I could care for Mom without taking time off work. Helping her with the bedsore was a humbling experience for both of us, but it brought us closer together. I knew God was at work in our relationship. With his great humor, Dad made the time special, too. We would sit in the rocking chairs in my living room, rocking and talking for hours. When the ice storm cleared, Mom and Dad returned home.

In May 2009, tragedy struck. Charlene was diagnosed with brain cancer and passed away shortly after. Her husband, Mike, decided that Mom and Dad could no longer stay in the house, so they had to move. When Dad asked Mom where she wanted to live, she chose Nebraska, where she was originally from. My two older sisters, Pat (in South Dakota) and Nancy (in Nebraska), along with two nephews and a niece, flew to New Hampshire to help pack up and move Mom and Dad. I joined them for the packing, and we finished everything in one day. Mom and Dad flew with my sisters while the men drove the rental truck to Nebraska.

It was bittersweet to see them leave, but I was grateful for the time we had together. In October 2009, I visited my sister Nancy in Nebraska for the first time. I met my sister Pat and brother Henry and reconnected with my brother Jim, who had moved out west years ago. I only saw my mom once more before she passed away in 2011.

God is truly the God of restoration, and I thank Him for my time with my mom before she left this earth. Now, I move forward with the rest of my story.

CHAPTER EIGHT

Death of My Husband Francis

"But I would not have you to be ignorant, brethren, concerning them which are asleep, that ye sorrow not, even as others which have no hope. For if we believe that Jesus died and rose again, even so them also which sleep in Jesus will God bring with Him."
– 1 Thessalonians 4:13-14 KJV

As I mentioned before, my husband, Francis, had many health issues throughout his life.

Yet, the Lord carried us through every trial. Fran believed in the Lord, but he was quiet about his faith. When he was 12, he attended a Baptist church in Lebanon, Connecticut, where he received a Bible. His mom had divorced his dad because of abuse, and when she moved with her four sons, they stopped attending church.

After we married, Fran occasionally went to some of the churches I attended, but for the most part, he wasn't involved. We often took Fran's mom and stepdad out to eat on Saturdays. After Fran's mom passed, we continued this routine. While Fran was driving one afternoon, his stepdad sat in the front, and I was in the back seat. As I stroked Fran's hair, he glanced at me through the rearview mirror with his beautiful blue eyes and a gentle smile. At that moment, I felt the Lord's still, small voice in my spirit: "He won't be with you much longer." Those words saddened me deeply. Fran was about 64 then, and his heart was weak. He didn't want another heart surgery.

Fran began showing interest in returning to the Baptist church in Lebanon, though he didn't mention much to me. He would stop to check service times when we drove by but didn't want me to know he was attending. I later found out when we ran into one of his cousins at the Lebanon Fair, and she asked if she'd see him at church on Sunday. The secret was out! I didn't bring it up immediately but kept attending my church.

One night, I had a dream. Fran and I were in a small plane, and he was the pilot. It was a bright winter day, and the ground sparkled with pure white snow. Looking out the window, I saw a church surrounded by a joyful community dressed warmly and looking up at us. The dream ended, and I didn't fully understand it then.

Shortly after, as Easter approached, I felt the Lord tell me, "I want you to go to church with your husband." On Easter Sunday, I asked Fran if I could join him at his church. He seemed surprised and asked, "Why do you want to go with me?" I told him it felt like that's where I belonged, and he agreed. From then on, I attended church with Fran. We went every Sunday, got to know the pastor and congregation, and were set to start greeting people as a couple on July 31, 2011.

In late July, my mom passed away suddenly. I flew to Nebraska to be with my stepdad and sister, leaving on July 27th and planning to return on Sunday. While I was gone, Fran worked long hours in the heat, helping a neighbor build a stone wall. The weather was sweltering, and it took a toll on his heart. I often prayed that God would either heal him completely or take him quickly to avoid more suffering.

When I returned on Sunday afternoon, Fran had already attended church and greeted without me. I was a bit disappointed to have missed it. Over the next few days, Fran continued working after his job. On Tuesday night, I felt uneasy in my spirit but didn't know why. The next day, Fran left for work as usual. I went to work and then visited a nursing home. As I was leaving that afternoon, I received a call saying Fran was in the emergency room in Marlborough, Connecticut. I quickly got in my car and headed there, even though I wasn't in the best state to drive. Minutes from reaching the ER, I was involved in a serious accident. By God's grace, I walked away unharmed.

When I arrived at the ER, I learned Fran had passed away. My heart was heavy, it was not easy emotionally. God was holding me together. I called my children, and they came to support me. My youngest son, Joseph, took it the hardest. He had hoped for a closer relationship with his dad.

We decided to hold Fran's memorial service on Sunday, August 7th, at the Lebanon Baptist Church. The church was packed with family and friends, overflowing with love. Reflecting on my dream of the plane and the church, I realized God had prepared me for this moment. Fran left a legacy of kindness and love; I know he's with Jesus now. One day, I will see him again.

The promise in Revelation 21:4 gives me comfort: *"And God shall wipe away all tears from their eyes; and there shall be no more death, neither sorrow, nor crying, neither shall there be any more pain: for the former things are passed away."*

CHAPTER NINE

Widowhood

Now she that is a widow indeed, and desolate, trusteth in God, and continueth in supplications and prayers night and day.   Timothy 5:5 KJV

When my husband Francis passed away on August 3, 2011, it was on our 43rd anniversary. I thank the Lord that I reached the age to qualify for widow's benefits. I was 59 and a half years old. I had lost my job at the school two years earlier and was working as a caretaker, but my income wasn't enough to cover the cost of utilities, taxes, and upkeep on our home. Francis didn't have life insurance, which made things even harder.

Not long after his passing, a real estate agent tried to take advantage of me, offering a very low price for my home. I could not believe that there were people who would take advantage of a widow. I refused and sent him away. It was overwhelming thinking about selling Francis's tools, tractors, and equipment. We still owed money on our home and had other debts. I also had to decide which vehicle to keep. Since my car had higher payments, I chose to sell it.

I decided to stay in our home for one more year. My son Joseph took on the responsibility of selling items from the workshop. I eventually put the house up for sale and found a buyer who paid enough to cover all the debts. I sold the house in October 2012, 14 months after Francis's death. With help from a close friend, I packed up and moved out. I stored a few things I thought I'd need for the future and rented a room in someone's home until the Lord showed me the next step.

I stayed in Connecticut, living in the countryside. I helped with chores like shoveling snow, carrying firewood, and cutting the lawn—things I would have done if I still owned a home. It was a place where the Lord taught me how to live in His peace despite challenges. The woman I rented from and I had some good times together, but living with someone used to being alone wasn't always easy, and adjustments had to be made on both sides.

During this time, I visited my sons and babysat my grandchildren. I stayed in that home from November 2012 to April 2014. When it was time to move again, I didn't know where to go. I wrote out a prayer, reminding the Lord of His promises:

- *"But seek ye first the kingdom of God, and his righteousness; and all these things shall be added unto you"* (Matthew 6:33 KJV).
- *"But my God shall supply all your need according to his riches in glory by Christ Jesus"* (Philippians 4:19 KJV).

I applied for housing in various places and found a small East Hampton, Connecticut community. To live there, you had to be 62 years old or handicapped. I turned 62 in March 2014, and the Lord opened the door for me to move in. It was a small, efficient apartment, just right for me, with a bedroom, a good-sized bathroom, a walk-in shower, and a kitchen/living room combo. I called it my "prayer closet" because I would sit in my prayer chair, look out the window at the sky, and spend hours in prayer and intercession. God's faithfulness provided me with a quiet and restful place.

While living there, I helped some of the residents. I fed a neighbor who couldn't feed herself when her caretaker didn't show up. I took others grocery shopping and shared the love of Jesus with them. One widower, who wanted to place roses on his wife's grave in Vermont, felt discouraged because the weather made the trip impossible. I comforted him by saying his wife would understand and reminded him of Jesus's love and compassion. He felt better and even gave me a couple of roses.

Not everyone appreciated my faith, and some called me a "Bible thumper." I didn't let it bother me. I explained that a relationship with the Lord isn't about keeping rules but walking in His love. Over time, I learned *faith is a rest*—trusting that God will do what is best for us. If we do our part, He will do His.

In 2017, I started attending a home meeting called, Mountain of Worship where they taught about the gift of prophecy. I met people who wanted a deeper relationship with the Lord. The worship drew us into sweet, intimate times with Him, and we shared what He revealed. I formed friendships that felt closer than family.

In August 2022, while babysitting my grandsons, I slipped on a toy and broke my hip. The surgery went well, but rehab was challenging. Some staff were kind, but one therapist pushed me too hard, making recovery painful. With the Lord's help and support from friends, my fellowship group, and church. I recovered and was thankful to be able to walk again.

I joined an online prayer group through the School of the Holy Spirit during this time. We prayed daily and studied topics like prophecy, priesthood, and dream interpretation. The Lord opened the door for me to become a prayer leader and even teach, which was humbling. One of my leaders often asks, "Are you available?" My answer is always yes!

The Lord wants to use each of us for His glory. As 1 Peter 4:10-11 (KJV) states "*As every man hath received the gift, even so, minister the same one to another, as good stewards of the manifold grace of God... that God in all things may be glorified through Jesus Christ.*"

CHAPTER TEN

Death Of My Two Son's Luke and Joseph

Fear thou not; for I am with thee: be not dismayed; for I am thy God: I will strengthen thee; yea, I will help thee; yea I will uphold thee with the right hand of my righteousness." Isaiah 41:10-KJV

This part of my life's story is bittersweet. Luke had been in a care facility, MHCC, for nearly 10 years. In 2019, I had a dream or vision where I saw myself in heaven. In the vision, Jesus was sitting on a magnificent golden throne. He wore a pure white robe with a beautiful purple sash and held a golden scepter in His right hand. Jesus pointed the scepter at my son, Luke, who stood before Him. He then spoke, saying, *"Healing granted!"*

I believed that I would see Luke healed here on earth, but that wasn't God's plan. In September 2022, Luke started eating less and began to lose weight. The nurse and I noticed this change, and I became more vigilant about monitoring his meals. I urged the staff to give his medications after his meals so he might eat more, but despite my efforts, his condition worsened. I repeatedly asked for his medication doses to be reduced, as they seemed excessive, but the neurologist only added more. It was difficult to find a new doctor willing to take on Luke's case.

One day, the nurse caring for Luke gently told me that he had lost 14 pounds in just two weeks and that he likely had only a few months left. While I hoped for a turnaround, I remembered my vision of Jesus and prayed for a miracle. But God had other plans.

Let me pause here and share a story about my son Joseph.

One autumn day, I was visiting friends in my hometown, Lebanon, Connecticut. The weather was perfect, with colorful fall leaves, open green fields, and a bubbling brook nearby. I felt so close to God that day. I spent the afternoon reminiscing and enjoying the beauty of nature. That night, I went to bed full of peace and gratitude.

Around midnight, I was suddenly awakened by a call from Joseph, my youngest son. He was at the hospital ER and being admitted. He'd been in pain all day and decided to get checked out on his way home from work. I quickly got dressed and went to be with him. When I arrived, Joseph was in terrible pain.

I stayed with him through the night, praying constantly. By the next afternoon, the doctors informed us that Joseph had small cell cancer in his right lung. My daughter-in-law Jen, along with my grandchildren Aydin and Ivy, came to visit. It was an incredibly difficult time for our family. I continued praying for Joseph and for God's healing.

Over the next month, I found myself traveling back and forth between visiting Luke and Joseph. Luke's facility was only seven miles away, but Joseph was an hour's drive. I tried to make Joseph's days a little brighter, bringing him his favorite pastries as long as he could enjoy them. I also babysat my grandchildren so Jen and Joseph could attend appointments.

During this challenging season, I held tightly to God's promises. A verse that brought me comfort was John 14:27: *"Peace I leave with you, my peace I give unto you: not as the world giveth, give I unto you. Let not your heart be troubled, neither let it be afraid."*

Now, back to Luke's story.

Luke's health continued to decline. We tried offering soft, easy-to-eat foods, but he ate very little. I visited him daily, knowing how hard this was for him and for our entire family.

On Thanksgiving Day, November 25, 2022, I was sitting in my prayer chair, looking out the window. I saw two male cardinals sitting side by side on a tree branch. I had never seen two cardinals so close before. In my heart, I felt the Lord say, *"These two cardinals represent your sons, Luke and Joseph."* When one cardinal flew away, I heard, *"Luke will leave first."* The other stayed a little longer, and I heard, *"Joseph will remain for a while."*

This was a confirmation to me that the Lord was speaking. Though my heart was heavy, I believed He was sparing them from the trials ahead.

On December 22, 2022, at 3 a.m., I got a call that Luke could pass at any moment. I went to the facility immediately. My pastor, my son Shane, and my friend Susan and her husband Ernie came and visited with us. My dear friend Susan and I said goodbye, singing *"Amazing Grace"*. At 11:30 p.m., Luke went home to Jesus.

We held a memorial service for Luke, surrounded by friends and family. Their love and support meant so much to me. A verse that brought me comfort during this time was Proverbs 18:24: "A man *that hath friends must show himself friendly: and there is a friend that sticketh closer than a brother."*

Meanwhile, Joseph's condition worsened. He was in constant pain, and chemotherapy wasn't helping. His appetite disappeared, and he lost weight rapidly. Jen took on the role of caregiver, and it was a tough time for the entire family.

A week before Joseph passed, he called me with a special request. He asked me to record his words: *"My dearest mommy, this is your boy, and he wants to tell you he loves you so very very much. And he will miss you, and he will see you on the other side. And will wait for you. Please, please understand that I forgive for every stupid thing or anything that you think would hold me. I love you so very, very much."*

Joseph passed away on July 4, 2023, seven months after Luke. Though my heart aches for them, I find comfort in knowing they are with Jesus, along with my former husband.

A verse that strengthens me is 1 Corinthians 2:9: *"But as it is written, Eye hath not seen, nor ear heard, neither have entered into the heart of man, the things which God hath prepared for them that love him."*

People often ask how I made it through such a difficult time. I can only say it was God's amazing grace. There were moments of doubt, but I never lost trust in Him. He provided comfort through His word and the love and prayers of friends and family.

From September 2022 to July 2023, I went through this difficult time. I had support from my beloved friend Susan Noviello, who encouraged me to keep my eyes on Jesus and look to Him for comfort. My wonderful friend Doris Bailey was always there for me. I could call her anytime, day or night, to cry and find support.

God's word gave me strength, especially the verse: *"Let us therefore come boldly unto the throne of grace, that we may obtain mercy, and find grace to help in time of need."* (Hebrews 4:16, KJV).

The Mountain of Worship team, led by Danny and Karen Steyne, supported me with their love and prayers. The School of the Holy Spirit gave support at this time. My church helped me out. My friend Carol Eisenberg showed love by cooking meals for Joseph and his family.

Many friends came together to help during my son Luke's memorial service. Life goes on, even when we lose the ones we love. I miss my sons so much, but I thank the Lord that I am not trapped in grief or sorrow.

This life is only temporary, and I hold on to the promise that I will see them again in their glorified bodies. What an amazing, promise-keeping God we serve!

CHAPTER ELEVEN

A New Marriage and New Life

" *Whoso findeth a wife findeth a good thing, and obtaineth favour of the LORD.*" *Proverbs 18:22   KJV*

I never expected this chapter of my life to unfold the way it did. The Lord amazes me with His goodness and mercy. At that time, I wasn't looking for a husband or interested in finding one. I used to joke with my friends, saying, "I'm not going husband hunting!" But God had other plans.

I would sometimes tell the Lord what kind of man I would want if I ever remarried, though I never thought it would happen. As widows, we're often told that Jesus is the only husband we need.

I attended fellowship meetings on Tuesday evenings with The Mountain of Worship. One evening, Ken showed up, brought by a longtime friend, Rob. Rob knew my late husband because he worked for his dad.

A few weeks later, Ken looked at me and smiled. I felt embarrassed and thought, "What does he want?" Eventually, I went over to talk to him and learned his name. Week by week, we talked more. I prayed, "Lord, is this from You? If so, please give me peace."

In March 2023, we exchanged phone numbers and began talking about the Lord over the phone. Soon after, we met for coffee and a meal, and that's how our relationship started. We continued seeing each other at the fellowship meetings, and the Lord gave me peace, confirming it was His will.

My dear friend Susan had a dream where she saw Ken and me flying in a jet airplane, and that's exactly how it felt! By June 2023, after four months of dating, we got engaged. Together, we picked out our rings.

Luke had already passed, but Joseph was still with us. Ken and I visited Joseph and his family so

I could introduce them. Despite Joseph's health struggles, he was glad to meet Ken.

Joseph's message also included a heartfelt note about Ken and me, expressing his love and support for our relationship: "I hope things work out for you and your friend, very good! Because you need some companionship and some happiness in your life as well. And I hope you find a lot of happiness, and I love you so very, very much. And please, please understand that I forgive for every stupid thing or anything that you think that would hold me. I love you I don't care."

Those words will stay with me forever. God, in His grace, hears our hearts, not just our words. Joseph's loving spirit remains a blessing in my life.

Ken built a beautiful new home from January 2022 to January 2023. He invited me to see it, and I was amazed. He's a skilled carpenter and takes pride in his work, making the kitchen cabinets, furniture, and other pieces himself.

We set our wedding date for August 26, 2023. Ken's pastor agreed to officiate, and my dear friend Susan became my Maid of Honor. Ken asked Rob to be his Best Man, and my granddaughter Ivy was our Flower Girl.

Fifty guests joined us on our special day. My sister Nancy traveled from Nebraska to help with the decorations and spend time with me. Susan helped with my dress, accessories, and hair. I wore a lovely blue dress that Nancy had given me.

The wedding day was sunny and warm. A dear friend made a beautiful white cake with blue flowers, and the meal was catered. Before the wedding, I had to clean out my East Hampton, Connecticut apartment. It was a lot of work, but I sold or gave away most of my things, keeping only what I truly wanted.

Ken already had plenty of furniture, but we shopped for a few household items together. God has been so good to me, blessing me with a kind and generous man of God and we were growing spiritually and blending our lives.

Since our marriage, Ken has built a stunning mantle for the fireplace. He's also been working on his classic trucks, including a beautiful blue 1964 Chevy pickup and a bright red 1996 Chevy pickup in pristine condition. We enjoy riding in them, which brings back great memories. Ken is incredibly handy and able to fix almost anything.

Starting a new life with Ken has been an adjustment, including making new friends in our area. But with God's grace and staying in His presence, everything has been more manageable.

One scripture we try to live by is 1 Corinthians 13:4-7: "Charity suffereth long, and is kind; charity envieth not; charity vaunteth not itself, is not puffed up. Doth not behave itself unseemly, seeketh not her own, is not easily provoked, thinketh no evil; rejoiceth not in iniquity, but rejoiceth in the truth." KJV

CHAPTER TWELVE

In Conclusion

"The fear of the LORD is the beginning of wisdom: And knowledge of the holy is understanding. Proverbs 9:10 KJV

In this chapter, I will reveal some of the lessons and wisdom the Lord has given me. One of the most important things I've learned is the value of prayer and talking to God. Spending time with Him is wonderful. Through a relationship with God, we truly come to know Him, not just know about Him. I didn't fully understand this until later in life, but it's part of our journey.

Each of us has a unique life journey, and understanding God and His Word is vital. Some lessons are meant for us personally, while others are meant to be shared. God has created each of us with a specific purpose—whether in ministry, the marketplace, public service, or as homemakers. Whatever we do matters as long as God is at the center of it.

The Bible is our guide, described as "a lamp unto our feet and a light to our path." Jesus is revealed throughout the Old and New Testaments. Though some deny the truth of God's Word, the Lord prepared us for this. As 2 Timothy 3:16-17 says: *"All scripture is given by inspiration of God, and is profitable for doctrine, for reproof, for correction, for instruction in righteousness: That the man of God may be perfect, thoroughly furnished unto all good works."*

Jesus also prayed for His disciples and us in John 17:13-14: *"And now come I to thee; and these things I speak in the world, that they might have my joy fulfilled in themselves. I have given them thy word; and the world hath hated them, because they are not of the world, even as I am not of the world."* In verse 17, He prays, *"Sanctify them through thy truth: thy word is truth."*

I trust God's Word completely. I didn't pray as effectively as I did in my earlier years. Prayer is something we grow in over time. Looking back, I realize I could have avoided a lot of heartache if I had prayed with more understanding when raising my family. But in life, some answers don't come the way we expect.

When my son Luke was born with disabilities, it was unexpected. I did everything I could during my pregnancy—eating well, taking vitamins, and resting—but we live in a fallen world, and some things are beyond our control. When my son Joseph was 17, he had a terrible motorcycle accident just a week before his 18th birthday. His bike's brakes failed, and he went over the handlebars, landing on the road and sustaining severe injuries. He was in the ICU for two weeks, but God brought him through. After that, Joseph always deeply appreciated the Lord, knowing his life had been saved.

My oldest son, Shane, joined the Army at 18 after high school. He wanted to escape my controlling tendencies, which I now understand. When we try to control everything, it reveals our insecurity. But I've learned to trust God, as Proverbs 3:5-6 teaches: *"Trust in the Lord with all your heart; and lean not unto thine own understanding. In all thy ways acknowledge him, and he shall direct thy paths."*

Shane served in Desert Storm and now works at a school for deaf students, raising his two sons, Logan and Brody. In 2011, he had a severe car accident but walked away uninjured. In 2023, he had another accident, breaking his arm, leg, and collarbone. Yet again, God protected him and my grandson Brody, who walked away with only a bump on his head.

Through all this, I've learned the importance of a personal relationship with the Lord. He invites us to call on Him, as Jeremiah 33:3 says: *"Call unto me, and I will answer thee, and show thee great and mighty things, which thou knowest not."*

As a child, I welcomed Jesus into my heart, but I didn't fully understand what that meant until I was older. Over the years, I've realized that God's Word is our guide to living a whole life. Following His principles leads to blessings, even for those who don't fully follow Him.

One example of God's faithfulness came when I prayed for a horse. After giving a special offering every three years, God blessed me with Bobby, a beautiful appaloosa horse. She brought joy to me and others, and her story reminds me of Luke 6:38:

"Give, and it shall be given unto you; good measure, pressed down, and shaken together, and running over, shall men give into your bosom."

I've also experienced God's healing power. Once, while caring for an elderly client, I fell and dislocated my hip. In immense pain, I cried out to the Lord, and within a short time, my hip went back into place. The pain disappeared completely, showing me the truth of Isaiah 53:4-5: *"By His stripes, we are healed."*

Gratitude is another lesson God has taught me. Life's hurts had left me bitter and ungrateful, but God showed me how to forgive and embrace thankfulness. This opened the door to new blessings, including a new husband and home. Ephesians 5:20 reminds us: *"Giving thanks always for all things unto God and the Father in the name of our Lord Jesus Christ."*

I pray everyone experiences the joy of an intimate relationship with the Lord. It's not about religion or rules but about walking with Him in love and faith. If you don't have this relationship, call on Him as Jeremiah 29:12-13 says: *"Then shall ye call upon me, and ye shall go and pray unto me, and I will hearken unto you. And ye shall seek me, and find me, when ye shall search for me with all your heart."*

The Lord has blessed me beyond measure, and I pray He blesses you as you seek Him with all your heart.

About the Author

Susan Dalla Corte is a devoted follower of Jesus Christ, a committed intercessor, a joyful worshiper, and a seasoned Elder cherishing the blessings of her later years. Her journey with Jesus began at the age of seven. At 19, she joined a legalistic church, but later in life, when she encountered the Holy Spirit, her true transformation began. Her inspiring story unfolds in these pages, offering insights into her walk of faith. Susan is happily married to Ken, has one living son, Shane, and two loving daughters-in-law, and is a proud grandmother to four wonderful grandchildren: Aydin, Ivy, Logan, and Brody.

Send mail to the author:

Susan Dalla Corte

P.O. Box 325
Stafford Springs, CT 06076

8 Commitments for being a Spiritual Warrior

1. **Being a Royal Priest**
   o **Prioritize** the first commandment: <u>**Love the Lord**</u> with all your heart, soul, and strength. Then, follow the second commandment: **<u>love yourself</u>** first then **love others.**
   o Priests prioritize <u>safeguarding the Lord's presence</u> in their earthly tabernacle (body and soul) first, then ministering in the heavenly tabernacle (seated in the heavenly places (spirit)).
   o **Pray Daily** (especially contemplative prayer), Dedicate at least 2 ½ hours a day to prayer.

2. **Cultivate a lifestyle of obedience and worship, rooted in the fear of the Lord.** Make it a daily practice to worship, obey, and read the Word, specifically the Book of Revelation. Fellowship with other believers.
   O <u>worship the LORD in the beauty of holiness</u>: fear before him, all the earth. —*Psalms 96:9*

3. **Consecrate and be thankful (Fasted Lifestyle).** Regal Priests consecrate themselves in their earthly tabernacle, their bodies, as their daily living sacrifices (per Psalm 24 "ascend") and (per Psalm 15 "dwell") in the heavenly tabernacle. Being Living Stones; Building a Spiritual House; Offer Spiritual Sacrifices of Righteousness; Sacrifices of Trust; Renewing your Mind (1 Peter 2:5, Psalms 4:5).

4. **Pure religion and undefiled before God:** Embrace the responsibility of being a good citizen on Earth by helping the poor, the widows, and the orphans, and lay low (James 1:27).

5. **Honor, Serve and Give extravagantly:** Give to support the kingdom by sowing into those who have paved the way for you.
   o Give elders double honor. Priest offer gifts and sacrifices to the Lord and the people (*1 Timothy 5:17*). Support your spiritual leaders with your resources and service.

6. **Make Disciples**: Duplicate yourself and give everything you have to receive more (Matthew 28:19).

7. **Power Evangelism:** He sent them to <u>preach the kingdom of God</u> and <u>to heal the sick</u> (Luke 9:2).
   o Cleanse the lepers, raise the dead, cast out demons. Prophesy and Win souls.

8. **Lead: Royal Priests Teach & Judge, Sanctify** and act as **ambassadors of His forgiveness**.
   o Preach the Gospel of the Kingdom by Teaching, Prophesying, Healing the Sick, Raising the dead. Casting out demons. Release SOZO (Greek for Saved, Healed, and Delivered) .

Figure 1[1]

---

[1] Thierry Nakoa, *The Testimony of Jesus-Is the Spirit of Prophecy: School of the Holy Spirit Manual 3a* (Thierry Nakoa, 2024).

SchooloftheHolySpirit.Church

www.ingramcontent.com/pod-product-compliance
Lightning Source LLC
Chambersburg PA
CBHW060939120626
46557CB00003B/1066